ONCE UPON A MIDNIGHT...

*Once upon a midnight dreary,
    while I pondered, weak and weary,
Over many a quaint and curious
    volume of forgotten lore —*

ONCE UPON A MIDNIGHT...

UNNAMEABLE PRESS ATLANTA
1995

Death Takes a Friend © 1995 Virginia Baker; Falling, Yves Tanguy FEAR 1949 © 1995 Lee Ballentine; Sit for Prophecies of Love © 1995 M. Shayne Bell; Utopia © 1995 Fred Chappell; Satan is a Mathematician © 1995 Keith Allen Daniels; The White Worm, The Resurrection Man © 1995 James S. Dorr; I am Myself—What the Other Said Was True © 1995 Denise Dumars; Elegy © 1995 Denise Dumars & Don Webb; Minstrel, Feint © 1995 Wayne Edwards; To Love is to Die, The Suicide © 1995 S.K. Epperson; When it All Began © 1995 Robert Frazier; Bag Lady's Ghost, Time is a Closet, To Love the Dark © 1995 Janet Fox; Palmyria of the Thousand Columns, Capt. Royate Montgomery Writes Home © 1995 Thomas E. Fuller; The Old Warlock's Reverie © 1995 Neil Gaiman; Dream Wells, The Last Siren in My Life © 1995 John Grey; The Bride © 1995 Owl Goingback; Holocaust in Rosary, Judas Nailed His Mouth Open © 1995 Charles A. Gramlich; Fin de Siecle, Ghost of Anchises © 1995 Donald M. Hassler; Three Hags Around a Fire © 1995 Diane Hughes; One Crow Many Graves © 1995 Dwight E. Humphries; Birth of the Second (For Poe) © 1995 Jean Jones; Ghosts, Masque © 1995 Geoffrey Landis; Greetings Again the Stars the Wind the Dark, The Dreams Within His Dream © 1995 Michael N. Langford; Woodworks, The Day of Hitler's Birth © 1995 Lisa Lepovetsky; Reliquarian Heart © 1995 Sandra J. Lindow; Beaters in the Bush, Hanged Man, The Zombie Glass © 1995 David Memmott; Eumenides © 1995 Michael Mina; The Fortress at the End of Time © 1995 Gregory Nicoll; The Eyes of Love © 1995 Sheila O'Shea; Hoodlum Shadows © 1995 Peter Payack; The Kiss: Wounds in the Mouth, The Density of Death © 1995 Jonathan V. Post; In the Darkness of the Hour © 1995 Mark Rich; Grey Synaptical Time Lapse, Small Hands, Behavior Patterns © 1995 Jame A. Riley; Goddess From the Sea, Night Call © 1995 John B. Rosenman; The Lot © 1995 Wayne Allen Salee; Carving a Life, In the Schwarzwald © 1995 Lawrence Schimel; Blood-Crossed Lawyer © 1995 Margaret B. Simon; Jeffrey Dahmer, In Praise of Entropy, No Mercy © 1995 S.P. Somtow; By Nectarine Gate © 1995 Steve Sneyd; walk with monsters, walk alone © 1995 W. G. Stewart; The Dark at the Door, The Dead Who Do Not Sleep Under Green Street, Poe's Grave, Shreve House © 1995 Steve Rasnic Tem; The Monster's Mother, Morgaine Mournes the Loss of Lancelot © 1995 Mary A. Turzillo; Awakening, Her Locks © 1995 Scott H. Urban; Down & Away (My Queen), My Body Goes on Forever © 1995 G. Warlock Vance; Deposed, He Remembers Her on the Morning of His Death; Following Her Divorce © 1995 Rick Wilber; Mechanisms of the Secret Moon © 1995 Thomas Wiloch; The Elf King's Daughter © 1995 Jane Yolen.

Frontispiece illustration © 1995 Alan Clark; cover photograph & design © 1995 Jame A. Riley. All other information herein, as well as the book design © 1995 Unnameable Press, Atlanta, GA — All Rights Reserved.

First Edition, March **1995**

Published by **Unnameable Press**
   P.O. Box 11689
   Atlanta, Ga 30355-1689

Contents

Introduction 5
Poe's Grave — Steve Rasnic Tem 6
Greeting Again the Stars, the Winds, the Dark - Michael N. Langford. 7
Dream Wells — John Grey 8
Masque — Geoffrey A. Landis 8
Dark at The Door — Steve Rasnic Tem 9
Morgaine Mourns the Loss of Lancelot — Mary A. Turzillo 9
Utopia — Fred Chappell 10
Yves Tanguy FEAR 1949 — Lee Ballentine 12
To Love the Dark — Janet Fox 13
The Zombie Glass — David Memmott 14
Eumenides — Michael Mina 15
Carving a Life — Lawrence Schimel 16
The Elf King's Daughter — Jane Yolen 17
No Mercy — S. P. Somtow 18
Feint — Wayne Edwards 19
Goddess From the Sea — John B. Rosenman 20
The Bride — Owl Goingback 21
Her Locks — Scott H. Urban 23
walk with monsters, walk alone — W. G. Stewart 24
The Last Siren in My Life — John Grey 25
Ghosts — Geoffrey A. Landis 26
Mechanism of the Secret Moon... — Thomas Wiloch 27
Fin de Siécle — Donald M. Hassler 28
Palmyria of the Thousand Columns — Thomas E. Fuller 29
Small Hands — Jame A. Riley 30
The Fortress At the End of Time — Gregory Nicoll 31
In Praise of Entropy — S. P. Somtow 32
Time as a Closet — Janet Fox 32
Grey Synaptical Time Lapse — Jame A. Riley 33
Woodworks — Lisa Lepovetsky 34
Shreve House — Steve Rasnic Tem 35
I am myself — What the others said was true — Denise Dumars 36
Three Hags Around the Fire — Diane Hughes 37
Sit for Prophecies of Love — M. Shayne Bell 38
Hanged Man — David Memmott 39
Birth of the Second (for Poe) — Jean Jones 40
The Lot — Wayne Allen Sallee 42
Bag Lady's Ghost — Janet Fox 43

Elegy— Denise Dumars & Don Webb 44
Behavior Patterns — Jame A. Riley 45
The Hoodlum Shadows — Peter Payack 46
Following Her Divorce — Rick Wilber 47
To Love is to Die — S. K. Epperson 48
The Eyes of Love — Sheila O'Shea 49
Deposed, He Remembers Her
   On the Morning of His Death — Rick Wilber........................... 50
Minstrel — Wayne Edwards 52
Death Takes a Friend — Virginia Baker 52
Beaters In The Bush — David Memmott 54
The Old Warlock's Reverie — Neil Gaiman 56
The Kiss: Wounds in the Mouth — Jonathan Vos Post 57
Awakening — Scott H. Urban 58
Holocaust In Rosary — Charles A. Gramlich 58
Reliquarian Heart — Sandra J. Lindow 60
Judas Nailed His Mouth Open — Charles A. Gramlich 61
The Day of Hitler's Birth — Lisa Lepovetsky 62
In the Schwarzwald — Lawrence Schimel 62
The Density of Death — Jonathan Vos Post 63
By Nectarine Gate — Steve Sneyd 63
Satan is a Mathematician — Keith Allen Daniels 64
Blood-Crossed Lawyer — Margaret B. Simon 65
The Resurrection Man — James S. Dorr 66
The Monster's Mother — Mary A. Turzillo 67
The Dead Who Do Not Sleep
   Under Green Street — Steve Rasnic Tem 68
The Ghost of Anchises: a Poem — Donald M. Hassler 69
Captain Royate Montgomery Writes Home — Thomas E. Fuller........ 70
Down and Away (My Queen) — G. Warlock Vance 71
Night Call — John B. Rosenman 72
When It All Began — Robert Frazier 73
Jeffrey Dahmer — S. P. Somtow 78
Falling — Lee Ballentine 78
My Body Goes on Forever — G. Warlock Vance 79
The Suicide — S. K. Epperson 80
In The Blindness of the Hour — Mark Rich 80
The Dreams Within His Dream — Michael N. Langford 81
The White Worm — James S. Dorr 84
One Crow, Many Graves — Dwight E. Humphries 86

Fantastic Terrors Never Felt Before
an introduction

"See! Hear! The Unnameable Traveling Poetry Road Show: Tripping The Dark Fantastic!"
Thus, through the instigation of playwright/poet Tom Fuller, your three humble editors — in fashions somewhat hammy, slightly Bradburian, often impassioned, at times Lovecraftian, yet ever dark and always Poe-inspired — came together in once-a-month readings of our own dark verse amid the bemused coffee-shop patrons of a local Atlanta bookstore.

"Hey, let's really take this thing on the road!" said DJ/poetry-slammer Mike Langford. But better yet, as originally conceived by Tom and book editor, Betsy Saunders within the stacks of still another bookstore, we decided to take our passions to press — Unnameable Press and its art director and publisher, poet Jame A. Riley.

The invitation for submissions then went out to the finest and darkest poets we could find. "Send us your grim, ungainly, ghastly, gaunt and ominous words of yore," we implored. And the quaint and curious verses arrived by the score, making this volume of all new poems a true celebration of the one-hundred-fiftieth anniversary of perhaps the most famous American poem and the cornerstone of all dark Romantic verse, Edgar Allan Poe's "The Raven".

We shall be grateful evermore to all those bards who submitted their shadowy lines. Special thanks goes to Elizabeth A. Saunders for her editorial and formatting expertise as well as her patience; to Margaret B. Simon and Robert Frazier for vital suggestions and leads; to Victoria A. Dufresne and Berta P. Fuller for indispensable inspiration and patience; to Brian & Andria Berkley for hospitality and laser printers; to Neil Avery III, raven wrangler/choreographer; and, of course, to our coverbird, nameless here forevermore.

So here we open wide the door and offer these mysteries to explore. Deep into this darkness peering, you may hear faint foot-falls on the tufted floor. If so, your soul from out these shadows may be lifted — Nevermore!

Poe's Grave
Steve Rasnic Tem

He is not dead.
He only sleeps: his hair
as long as fear, as old
creeping into the blind
dark hearts underground
we forgot were there.
His eyes are stones
and too large for the skull;
there is terror in vision
that sees far more than words
will tell. Our children
compel us to bury him
again, for peace, again,
for a good night's sleep.
But he will not stay. Buried
fingers, tongue, his stare
cough up with each dream.
He is not dead,
but only sleeps,
and with each terror
unspoken, he walks.

Greeting Again the Stars, the Winds, the Dark
Michael N. Langford

Under raging wilds that beat and blow
each ragged point of light, nailed
so sure and deep in that eternal, ebon breast,
I stand, at once and forever,
a child with unclouded brow, buffeted
to momentary tears, thrown
across blistered cheeks from air-burned eyes,
across battered sense from fire-parched sight of
six-thousand stellar stoves.

Blown, blasted, and breathless, I hold
fast beneath each wonder-worked and mystery-made
slice of night-flow and far-light,
ever shearing off and spilling down —
with no knowable rest —
from every mind-baking world-oven
and rushing wail of thought there is.

I smile and greet again
each brilliant wind,
each biting star,
each sharp and flying thing
ever flung across the old, soft dark
so much beyond yet much within me.

Dream Wells
John Grey

Begin the humming choir of sleep,
Weigh down those eyes, these lissome lids,
My mind peers down through nameless grids
Into the dream wells, dug so deep,
And from the murmur of my bed,
I float down, down, and never stop
Until the bottom and the top
Are polarized inside my head,
Like two streams in the same canal,
The waking and the wanting to,
The aching and the what I do,
The common and unusual.

Masque
Geoffrey A. Landis

In times of brief, bright passion
at full intensity
we forget our masks and mirrors,
the things we feign to be

and only in remembering
much later, do we see
that at the edge of living —
in death and love — we're free.

Dark at The Door
Steve Rasnic Tem

He found no cure
for the dark at the door,
no help for the wolves,
or the birds, raving
through the endless sleep
where he walked with lost lovers,
and a thread of music
only he could hear: the tortured
sprung of worlds turning
when what he loves, dies,
filling the moon
with amber.

Morgaine Mourns the Loss of Lancelot
Mary A. Turzillo

They do not come back, blue lady,
lost lovers. Nor all your spells and charms,
clever gifts or soft green eyes will bring them.
Therefore think of him only as the flash
of silver in the ring you lost
over the rowboat's side one golden autumn
as it sank swiftly through the water.
And if it ever comes to womankind again
from down among the cattails where it lies,
it will be to ornament another woman's hand,
in the far future, in some other land.

Utopia
Fred Chappell

Above the doorway over there,
Just to the left of the hanging crocodile,
We see a painting clouded dark with grime —
Mist-hazy, hovering in stale air —
That offers a vision of some future time
Or maybe of a past no one remembers.

The painter's style
(If such a muddle can be termed a style)
Is so ambiguous that everyone
Who peers closely into
Those sweeps and swirls, those surf-spray brushstrokes,
Clouds of violet, tumults of star-flecked blue
And dripping emerald, that dun-orange blot of dying sun,
Finds momentary figures in the arabesques
Of mauves and saffrons and somber umbers.

It is the picture of Utopia: we all agree
Upon its major subject. Even so,
Where one observer finds a meadow of bees and daisies
Another finds a sea
Silent with twilight and a perfumed sky.
Some men see Woman, women may see a man.
Some see a metropolis with mazes
Of shady alleys leading off a mile-wide avenue
That leads to a marble Temple of the Sun.
Everyone seems to see Somewhat —
Or almost-see —
But cannot say, and yet can almost-say
The melting figures and streaming images
Of this Better Thing that was or maybe shall be but never is,
Yet pours its radiance upon our thought.

In dreams we stretch our hands to clutch
Forms that turn our flesh to ghost,
Cancelling its power to hold, even to touch,
The luminous shadows that possess it most:
Like these, the images that this oil portrays
In colors that dislimn the outlines
That are not boundaries,
With modeling that shapes no models,
With chiaroscuro that defines
Neither light nor dark with spotless
Volumeless surges of dim improbable hues.

The painting shows us another world, another kind
Of world, different from the ravaged town,
The burning orphanage and rubbled sanitorium,
The heart struck dumb,
Head seared blind,
The highest courage beaten down:
Every detail that makes our world our own
As real as shrapnel. A different kind
Of world, we murmur. Yet we agree
This painting stands behind
The daily ruin we accept as our reality.

Pictor ignotus, the experts say.
Painter unknown.

...on this desert land enchanted —

Yves Tanguy FEAR 1949
Lee Ballentine

How near is the delirium of vapor
that's knitted from the summer rain?
Past your confusion of lilacs.
Past that shadow in the shape of a wolf
following you. Last night a tiger drowned
and tonight I swim the sea of Cortes
eating the flesh of the wind.

In dreams on my barge I accuse myself
of the crime of your vacant house
its doors swinging wildly
as winged men bathe
in whirlpools in their armor
cold water warping down their throats
would rust the mechanisms of sexless fishes.

But my love is Yves Tanguy FEAR 1949.
She holds up her breasts with ribbons of genocide.
She rolls—silent on the bed of clear ice
she slumbers on.

To Love the Dark
Janet Fox

Let me sing the song
Persephone learned
far below in uncharted night,
winding her way in labyrinthine darkness
with sunlight a fading memory.
Let all edges be softened by shadow;
proceed in darkness,
cast myself down in cool, winecolored grass
where asphodels hang pallid heads
shining like mushrooms in clinging dark.
Let silence be poured, a balm
into my brain.
Those who fretted away meager lives
approach and then, as if through mist
perfumed with indefinable scent,
I pass through them, entering
an inner chamber where my Lord
is statue-like upon his throne.
His eyes are hooded, what must it be
to look into them?
His bleak lips smile;
he extends a hand, blunt-fingered, steady —
no one slides from that clasp.
I sing the old song Persephone taught me.
In time one learns
to love the dark

The Zombie Glass
David Memmott

Welcome to the ranks of the living dead.
From here on, only one road and it narrows to a point.
We meet each morning in the Zombie Glass
to meld our separate selves into one cold essence.
From now on, your time is my time
- reflect that well.
You are now worth this much an hour.
Through your heavy-lidded, half-open eyes
all value can be reduced to things
and all things are worth this much.
My purpose is to document your slow decline,
your inevitable and purgatorial surrender.
Watch me in the Zombie Glass
become you as you become me, become we.
Join us here on the other side.
Replayed in our reanimated eyes is a history of hurt.
We feasted on suffering; now your pain sustains us.
Chew on disappointment, grind your teeth;
sooner than later, the transformation will be complete.
We will merge in rains of regret, born into bitterness.
From the Hall of Mirrors and its probable selves,
you hand picked me to darkly represent you here.
So welcome to the kingdom of strict accounts.
We will mark yours well.

Eumenides
Michael Mina

As I knelt beside the shore of the Lethe,
Eumenides, falsely named, attending,
I drew the waters into my mouth, but did not swallow,
fearing the fugue, and arose to face them.

I thought of those I had loved and lost,
and those I had left behind, mourning.
A daughter, a son, a wife, all dear.
I recalled the fresh scents of spring
as the reek of dying asphodels filled the air.

And I wondered why gods so-called would have it thus.
The only treasures one may carry beyond are memories,
yet they would take these from Man as well,
that not even the mind's eye might gaze on aught but Erebus.

They laughed at the cries of my mourners,
Hectate's hounds that mocked my mortality,
these foul abortions of Earth, steeped in blood,
unworthy of Olympus.

I spewed the black water into their accursed faces,
black water to mix with the blood that rains ever from their eyes.
No, I decided as they tore at my flesh, I would face their
      unyielding fury.
It were better to scream unto the end of days than ever to forget.

Carving a Life
Lawrence Schimel

The pumpkin sits heavy in your lap.
You trace the lumpy folds of its face
with your fingertips, feel its bad skin,
the orange knobs like pimples, the extra chins.

You feel so much sympathy for it;
you feel so much like this ugly squash.

You have been waiting for it
to transform into a coach
and carry you away in glass slippers.
The barn is full of rats for coachmen.
You'd even drive it yourself,
the reins in your now thin, pale hands,
the prince at your side.

Is a coach too much to ask for?
The pumpkin is the color of your tractor
and you'd gladly ride it into the sunset
if only you were beautiful.

But you are tired of waiting for impossible dreams,
for faery glass slippers and pumpkins
with four wheel drive.
You will carve a beautiful face tonight.
You lift the knife from beside you on the porch,
hold out your wrist,
and carve a jack-o-lantern
from the drab, orangish flesh,
from your bad skin, thick as a pumpkin rind
with the callouses of work.

Its eyes are bright red
all through the long night.

The Elf King's Daughter
Jane Yolen

When he first saw her
She was drinking wine,
Her skin so pale
He could trace the path of it
Down her throat.
His mouth filled as if tasting
The rich full body
Though he had not yet brought
Cup to lips.

When she looked at him
He drank, the amber and the red,
Making his stay in Faerie
Nine times nine.

When they were done with him
He lay on the hillside,
Old, drained,
The print of her lips
On his whitened neck
So finely etched,
As if she had sucked
All ten pints of him
In a single draught.

No Mercy
S. P. Somtow

There are no knights-at-arms, you say;
    There is no cold hill's side;
The concrete stretches to the sea.
    And the grass has died —

But you are wrong to tell me, friend,
    That faeries are no more.
They stand and beg for taxi-fare
    By the grocery store —

And, when you gaze too hard, too long
    Into their listless eyes,
You too can know those shabby shapes
    Are a shrewd disguise —

Because you did not wish to see
    Hear, smell, touch, tarry, taste
The strange seduction in those eyes,
    You slunk in haste

Back to the asphalt hinterland
    Back to the stucco grot,
Where space is personal, and time
    Fits in a slot —

They did not lull you with their song;
    You only lulled yourself;
Your apathy concealed the nature
    Of the Elf —

No kisses four. No nightmare faces
    Out of the primal deep;
You lay undreaming in the arms
    of Prozac® sleep —

Did you not wonder whether it were
    Wiser to be unwise? —
To brave the white trash wilderness
    Behind those eyes?

Never? Then cruise the concrete night,
    Friend, find your faery bride —
For your lost spirit yearns to founder
    On that cold hill's side.

Feint
Wayne Edwards

at last the whisper comes
the last attempt at life
her body smoothes in the giving

I pretend for a while she's not dead
hold her paling hand watch
for a twitch a sign a siege

I feint forgiveness then damn
her soul for giving in
for trusting death to salve her pain

I remain to host her vision
memory's sentinel entombed
far more tightly than she

Goddess From the Sea
John B. Rosenman

(This poem is based upon Thomas Mann's **Death in Venice**. Just before he dies, Gustave Aschenbach, who is tormented by his erotic obsession for an exquisitely beautiful boy named Tadzio, sees Tadzio emerge from the sea.)

Goddess from the sea!
An angel's smile of mischief madness
stirs his sadness, makes it all.

On the beach
the old man sips
cool pomegranate-juice,
kissing distorted visions
through darkening glass.
Alabaster arms stroke
the languid frenzy of his brain
and golden curls
toss careless splendors
in a dazzling rain.

Death's eye watches
and flutters once against the sun.
The tripod tumbles,
and dead-ripe strawberries
melt one by one.

The Bride
Owl Goingback

A foghorn echoes through the darkness of night
Calling lovers home from the sea.
Maybe if the foghorn sounds loudly enough,
It will bring back my Sarah to me.

Such is the dreams of heartsick old men
Who have had their lovers stolen away.
But the dead remain dead, never to walk again.
No matter how hard you pray.

Ah Sarah, my Sarah, she was such a beautiful lass,
With a heart as good as they came.
She filled my life with happiness,
And gave me shivers when she whispered my name.

We were engaged to be wed, Sarah and I
Back in the summer of '62.
I remember the season well. The sun was so bright,
And the sea a glorious blue.

But the sea is also a woman, and jealous as sin.
Every sailor knows this to be true.
She resented Sarah's beauty and my happiness,
And knew just what to do.

We were out in a small boat, Sarah and I
Maybe a mile or more from the shore.
The day started calm, but a storm sprang up
And the wind did begin to roar.

The sky grew as black as a banker's heart
And our boat was tossed about on the waves.
"Cling Tight, my love" I yelled to Sarah
As we raced to escape a watery grave.

Now the sea she did howl as we headed for shore,
For she knew we were getting away.
But the fight was far from over,
For she had one more trick to play.

From out of the ocean sprang a towering wave.
A terrible sight to see.
A wave in the shape of a giant hand,
With fingers as big as a tree.

The wave, this wave, a watery hand, grabbed my
Sarah and tore her from me.
It swept her off the boat and carried her down
To a grave, deep beneath the sea.

Many a year has passed since that day.
Many a tear have I cried.
I remember the look of terror on the face
Of my beautiful future bride.

Well too I remember the sound that I heard
As Sarah was taken from me.
It was the sound of laughter, a woman's voice.
The laughter of the sea.

So I sit here each night, a brokenhearted old man.
Whose spirit is barely alive.
Wondering when I die who will come for me.
The sea or Sarah, my bride?

For the rare and radiant maiden...

Her Locks
Scott H. Urban

In solitude, she plaits her hair,
Her auburn, glowing, flowing hair.

The tresses spill around her face,
Fade into earth without a trace.

Pale, narrow fingers rise to comb
Out damp humus and dirty loam.

Medusa-like, her strands a-writhe,
Parody of being alive:

The only beauty she can save
In the cold and unfeeling grave.

In solitude, she plaits her hair,
Her auburn, flowing, glowing hair.

walk with monsters, walk alone
W. G. Stewart

I look into the face of Medusa
and wait, counting and counting over
those separate serpent strands, her hair,
with the minutes, ticking.

I stare into her face and wait
for the stone and cold, an adamant
that does not come, awkwardly.

I look into the eyes of Medusa and see
a thousand years — more really — alone
and uncompanioned; I see her dispassionate tears
pebbled in piles at her feet.

I stare into her eyes and find the reasons
that she wills me, not turn to stone, and see
her reasons are the reasons that *I* wish it.

The Last Siren in My Life
John Grey

The siren sings to tease and tame,
You melt the victim in your eye,
Pretend you do not hear that cry
Amid the dark fire of your game,
You fan the sad Medusa flame
But in the coffin of your sigh,
There comes a man who does not die,
Who does not burst upon your name.

And horror threads your wounded face
As you stand there with mane of snakes
Attempt to slander, to debase,
To make him pay for your mistakes,
But you are shrunk to common-place,
And nothing changes, nothing breaks.

Vretch," I cried, "thy God hath lent thee —"

Ghosts
Geoffrey A. Landis

And so you said good-bye. And so I went.
What did you fear? I fear I'll never know.

I've long made friends of ghosts of might have been.
still know that somewhere there are rivers still
and roads that wander under other stars;
I know one day I'll leave this place as well,
make changes and take chances once again.
I will, if not just yet, yet someday still.

A thousand years from now, or only ten
we'll both have grown, we'll both have traveled far;
once more be friends, together laugh again
at what, back then, we were, or might have been.

I'll linger with this world you've left me in;
for now, I'll live with ghosts of might have been.

Deep into that darkness peering...

Mechanism of the Secret Moon...
Thomas Wiloch

I.

Like glass petals unfolding, the mirror opens and she steps into the silent room. Her eyes are ecstatic ghosts; her fingers explore the softly-lit air. She spins curls of smoke into images of her wayward children. She lights the air with blossoming kisses which float in feathered luxury. She weeps as stars falls from the sky to form transitory silhouettes of the gods. She cuts her wrists and holds them out to me saying, "Drink this, for this is my blood." And I reach for her hand to drink as she bids me, but she is smoke, a memory, my hand passes through her and I cannot hold her close to me. "No," I beg her, "you cannot leave me again..." But, in soft eclipses of hollow angels, she steps back into the mirror and it closes shut behind her, gently, like a remembrance of dawn. And the room goes dark...

Outside, her children wander the night like pale vapor trails of forgotten comets.

II.

I opened my eyes to find veiled children weeping in this darkened room. The mirrors show images of burning cities, the floor is littered with fossilized hands, the echoing chimes of cathedral bells form prayers of enigmatic grace. The children turn to me, as if my presence offers them some hope, some chance for salvation. They stand; they reach out to me with eager fingers, like veiled deities dispensing a tentative blessing. "Are you my children?" I find myself asking, but this question only makes them weep louder. The black veils in front of their faces rock back and forth, touching the skin just beneath the cloth to form a vague and rippling topography. I back away from their many reaching hands, bump against a wall. They urge me into a corner, their blinded faces weaving before me, their insistant fingers prowling the air. "Are you my children?" I again demand. Their tiny hands touch me from many angles, pass through me, into me, and the children begin to enter me, walking into my body as I cringe and push at their ghostly shapes without effect. "Are you my children?" I cry again frantically. But the last child disappears into me without a word, the back of his head slowing for a moment before it sinks into my chest. And I am suddenly alone. The room is empty. The window shows a patch of night sky. Familiar traffic sounds can be heard in the street below. I catch my breath. It was only an illusion, a trick of the mind. These veiled children were never here. I never heard them weeping. That is when the mirrors flicker to life. That is when, in the mirrors' depths, I see dark figures, veiled, approaching me with tiny reaching hands.

The mirrors are filling with hands...

Fin de Siécle
Donald M. Hassler

I'm glad to have lived to see the end
Of centuries approach. Our grief
Can deepen with the fall and send
The winter messages as brief
And elegant as frozen pastorals
To save our child from horror that befalls.

Palmyria of the Thousand Columns
Thomas E. Fuller

Zenobia, warrior queen of desert sheltered Palmyria
Mistress of the Thousand Columns
Scourge of Great Rome
Humbler of Empires and Arrogant Men
Sits astride her midnight stallion
And watches the grey cavalry charge.

They thunder through the chest high grasses far below
Trampling it under stark steel hooves
Wounding the earth with the fury of their passage
Their sabers flash, lit with St. Elmo's Fire.
Their horns cry out like bronze bulls bellowing
And their undulating yells slice the air.

Their banners wave drunken above them
Blood red silks slashed twice with blue
Spangled with pentagram stars
Stolen from some unsuspecting night sky
They snap in the wind, adding their snarl
To the chorus of hoof and horn and yell.

Zenobia who fears no King or Emperor
Shudders in her silks and armor
She has watched them charge past
For six full days
And still the grass stands unbroken
And still they come again.

But beyond the curve of this fortress haunted mountain
Palmyria of the Thousand Columns waits
No longer defended by miles of empty sand
It lies naked on the featureless plain

A maiden staked out as sacrifice
To dragon minded phantom armies.

She has seen the wild grey riders charge
And she has seen the others
The cold knights of the sanguinary cross
The living metal castles and stalking things
The dark angels of the air
All ride endlessly to ravage Palmyria.

But none ever reach it.

And neither does she.

Small Hands
Jame A. Riley

The toys are dead.
Immobile on their shelves;
Somnolent in their boxes.
Their sound and motion
Have fallen away into time.
Small hands no longer
Grasp them or yank
Their strings. Small hands
Lost into the world.
The toys are dead;
Like forgotten fantasies, faded
Or trampled silently by
Time's passing footsteps.

The Fortress At the End of Time
Gregory Nicoll

A trapezoid of blackened stone
Rotating slowly, quite alone
Across a wine-dark sea of stars
Webbed with lichen, creased with scars
Once beckoned proud to warriors prime
This fortress at the end of time

Cannons cast from iron gleaming
Once coughed with flame and muzzles steaming
Crenelated towers tell
Where archers stood and swordsmen fell
Stains of rust sing songs sublime
In the fortress at the end of time

Skeletons of shattered bone
Softly 'neath the walls do moan
Of manticores and harpies' tooth
Tales of myth from tongues of truth
While spiders crawl o'er crusts of lime
In the fortress at the end of time

Forever flying 'cross the night
Ne'er to see the morning light
Its battlefields all lie behind
Decay now grows where armor shined
Doomed to dark for years of crime
The fortress at the end of time

In Praise of Entropy
S. P. Somtow

He warped out of some future Space and Time
And said: "'Tis wondrous, in this antique Land
That stone legs may stand trunkless in the Sand
And Transient Beauty is not deemed a crime
Evoking Public Censure. Where *I* live,
The Lifeless are Constrained to Permanence;
No sand may sift through Time's intemperate sieve.
Ten Thousand years, the Tall Titanium Tents
Remain unweathered by the Acid Rain.
Encased in force-fields, our proud Ziggurats
Will never shatter, for each window-pane
Is double-strapped with Diamantine slats.
How long, O Ozymandias, till the Earth
Learns this great truth: sans Death, there is no Birth?"

Time as a Closet
Janet Fox

Think of time
as a closet
with all your times
that were and could
have been intermingled
like outworn artifacts.
Real and unreal lie there
in a jumble, breathing dust,
waiting some unburial,
some final sorting.

All is well
if you can keep the door
firmly closed
but doors in unsteady
houses have a way of opening
a crack, standing
temptingly ajar

Grey Synaptical Time Lapse
Jame A. Riley

The streetlamp is distorted through
  Droplet covered glass. Spattered beams
Of light fall across my pages, dampening the
  Words with streetlight contortions.
The light through liquid crystal surface
  As the world... viewed through tears.
Tiny droplets impact on glass in silence.
  Far too small to be heard, only seen.
My thoughts mix with the
  Cool darkness and post midnight fog.
The edges fade as do the edges
  Of dreams; the edges of old antique
Photographs; the paint on my old car.
  Thoughts wander one a.m. streets,
Caught in the memories of cold
  Damp darkness. Memories lost,
But at home in the two a.m. fog.

Woodworks
Lisa Lepovetsky

Patient, vigilant,
we wait in houses for you.

Erect timbers moan your name
in their dirges
when grey winds violate
their despised chastity.
Paint peels like leprosy.
Windows are dark, alert,
coated with threads of time
and cobwebs as they
watch for your face.

No smoke escapes chimneys
choked by vines and magpies.
Doors riddled with long-deserted
wormholes swell in the rains,
warp in killing frosts,
hunger for your flesh
warm against their iron bolts,
bloodied with rust.

Inside, mahogany snakes
up stairs lying naked in the dusk.
Sunbleached roses wilt
on peeling wallpaper trellises.
Empty rooms echo rats' whispers
behind walls scarred in wars
with us when we still breathed.
Flies carpet dark corners
and mildew grows its
deformed flora on the ceilings.

We need you.
We wait for you to come home.

Shreve House
Steve Rasnic Tem

She came to see its gables clutch the moon,
so fierce she feared it choked the light away.
Then all night the seething sky keened off-tune.

Her husband toured her round the grand decay,
and claimed the house was tribute to his blood:
from the roof's cascade to the wide gateway,

he passed her through gravesites worried by flood,
halls and bedrooms alive with wretched gloom,
down to black cellars desolate with mud.

He was the man of her dreams, her dark groom,
whose vows of a life she need not suffer
made her his sculpture, then made this her tomb.

By promise and guile the mad man had her,
sired children and nightmares both to recur,
and this pleasing form he might disinter.

I am myself —
What the others said was true —
Denise Dumars

I am myself —
what the others said was true —
each summer has its end
the whippoorwills and mist

They say we came from Salem —
first —
reading Cotton Mather frightened me.
Oh how the night
has licked its wounds
and put away its sting!

Toward the end I stayed
around the house —
colors hurt my skin;
I could uncover nothing
that would explain
how I wished
for the cover of salt water!

And I longed for introduction —
"Miss Dickinson, fair Innsmouth!"

Ghastly grim and ancient...

Three Hags Around the Fire
Diane Hughes

Three hags around the fire
two lovers on the floor
six knitting needles clacking out
the clouds upon the moor.

A chalice, a church key,
two rabbits, a cat,
three candles for burning
the mad hatter's hat.

The stew within the cauldron
swallowed up the moon.
You handed me your matches.
They stood and called the rune.

The telephone was ringing.
Your hands controlled the word.
You pushed me in the cauldron
and pierced me with your sword.

So go your bloody way, love,
but leave the sword with me.
I'll float here midst our talismans

'til wounds begin to heal.

Sit for Prophecies of Love
M. Shayne Bell

I sit for prophecies of love
Beside locked doors, your doors
Seared red in sacrificial sunset —
Blood-smeared Moloch,
Burn my heart on ruthless altars:
   I bear it;
Rapt Delphic priestess, read dark oracles
Inside my chest torn open by your hands:
   I crave it;
Hot, fired love — I call it down,
I call it now, bewitched
By love, enraptured
By a sorceress' glare I dare not lose —
O! Witch of Endor, rise
From smoldering sands
To scorch my soul with love!

"Prophet!" said I, "thing of evil!"

Hanged Man
After Salvatore Rosa's SCENE OF WITCHES
David Memmott

With nightshirt billowing
a sailor's dream of silk,
you climb down off your meathook
to lead us through an ancient chant.
We all join in and peel our skin,
prick our eyes with steely pins,
but still no vision comes.

Nighthawks steal your last breath.
Below you, witches wait to clip your nails
and fumigate your hair. They stir your last rites
into poisonous brews, conjuring a bridge between worlds.
A sudden gust opens the way. You see the burning
creatures there at twilight edge of night.
They know you and you know them.

Up through fissures flow the dead
from cisterns and gutters where gravest matters
grow arms of spastic light. Subterranean eyes
fix you with a stare, introduce you into the tilting air.
Beached like a whale on some foreign shore,
you lie paralyzed as hungry natives speculate.
They poke your heaving sides with a stick
the jump back when your bloated belly splits.

Birth of the Second (for Poe)
Jean Jones

I

At the door of the library vista,
a ball filled with parading dancers.
Long trains of mourners follow
behind your eyes fluttering
towards the grandfather clock.
A dark coat, a short moustache.
We hear the bells chime.
It is
just as it was
during the first time.

II

When I was a child
alone at the park,
when I was nine and saw the hedges
for the first:
in my backyard with my G.I. Joes
and that remote-controlled tank:
I tossed you out on a parachute
and you cracked in two
against the sidewalk.

III

You were in Virginia's eyes
when I touched her for the first time.
You were Lea in the cemetery
when she sat naked by the tombstones.

You were Lisa, alone at Airlie after dark,
You were Susan doing somersaults
along the beach.

IV

You were the night
and all the things that wandered
in it through my mind:
Vampires, succubi, and other
women of the night:
that ten-year-old girl
who lived in the trailer
next to me
calling out my name,
the moon transformed
into a cigar-shaped cloud,

a crop of tentacles that erupted
from a slow, revolving sky
as I lay in bed alone
all alone waiting for you...

And each separate dying ember...

The Lot
Wayne Allen Sallee

for Lisa

Give me small reason for one more verse
Then let Lachesis dispose of her lot
And my words to the clouds will disperse
Worms hungry with glut will feed on my rot
Lost in mid-summer Remember When
And a billion lost seconds to bane
Cleansed in a hitched, rhyming tremble then
Bone tunes with sutures, red-foamed waved futures
Washed as with wet tears in rain
My only regret (once) with my death
A suspect wretched world would remain
The Gulf War, a diamond whore, reruns
Of Paris and Ilse and Blaine
Space shuttles exploded, St. Vitus devoted, and
The stutter of poets insane
Clotho, my friend, don't reveal me the end
Allow me to lathe one last line
Atropos can't rip me with her butcher's blend
And I shall conceive my penultimate time
Then leave my ashes to the Wabash River
And remit my grin to Perdition's last farm
So that Lisa, in a moment of fervor
Shall shudder at rumours of my cairn

Bag Lady's Ghost
Janet Fox

Fading in and out of intermittent
neon, the bag lady's ghost haunts
her corner, much as she did
when she was alive. Passersby
still don't see her as she
sits huddled in layers
of cast-offs, wrinkled and
discolored skin of face and
hands, only another layer,
quickly shed. I see her
from the window of my cafe
but only in the evenings
late, when I've had a drink
or two, so maybe
she's not there at all.
With the wind sweeping
along the street
sharp with cold,
though I can't feel it here,
I see her at her post
and wonder why she comes back
and back to this unkind moment
as if after whatever life
she may have had,
this was it for her,
poised on the edge
of bare survival
day by day; I can't imagine
whether it was tragedy or
triumph; maybe I'm happy
not to know.

Elegy
Denise Dumars & Don Webb

I have heard the chimes and flutes
Of secret places and cold spaces
That have never
Dreamt of man.

A dark breeze blows on me
That no one else can feel.
And I smell incense touched to flame
In honor of the dead.

They are gone, before
We even had a chance
To find them. As dead
As the poetry in poetry.

Should I sing to the bag lady
Of the Old Ones?
Can I raise my voice to the flower seller
And say, "We were not alone."?

What can I say of the star winds—
Save that I smell a little brimstone
In the air today,
Or maybe ozone from an unseen storm.

Behavior Patterns
Jame A. Riley

I've been stealing shadows
From strangers that walk
The sweltering streets of summer.
I wait until eleven o'clock
In the morning when
The shadows are small and
Snatch them and run home to
My cheap hole-in-wall apartment
Where I collect them all in a box
That I've marked:
"Darkness. Do Not Open!"

I take them all out at night
And watch them cavort about my
Dismal rooms. Darting in and out
Of the cracks and corners.
They whisper as they touch me.
I make a game of getting them
All back in the box before dawn.

...on the Night's Plutonian shore!

The Hoodlum Shadows
Peter Payack

Turning the clocks back
I forgot to reset the shadows.

So the shadows ran
an hour behind
all day long.

Once the sun went down
the shadows stood around
an extra hour,
loitering
like hoodlums on a street corner.

A shadow in the dark
looks like the negative
of a picture.

I called the cops
on the hoodlum shadows
for disturbing my peace of mind
with their shady shenanigans
and wise cracks.

By the time the cops
finally arrived,
the shadows had slipped away
into the darkness
like cat burglars who just robbed
an old man
of his visions of youth.

Following Her Divorce
Rick Wilber

Amy planted the seeds of her future
on a wet April Thursday under a gibbous moon
and a hope that soon he'd rise, erect,
from the garden soil and grow to be the man
she envisioned as hers.

Her thoughts were these —

He'd be cheap to feed and wouldn't read
when he could be making love.

He'd never run around and was certainly bound
to stay near his settled roots.

He'd be quiet at night and that was right
what she needed after her first husband's snore
that really, really wore her out.

He'd never, ever talk back,
and would fade with the frost,
which sounded like very nice timing,

though she considered the fact
that extra nitrogen and quite good loam
made such a perfect home that, well,

who knows what could happen come spring.
If it did that and a new man emerged
that might not be a bad thing either.

She could teach them all summer
about ornamentals, what to do,
how to look, what to think.

And just when each one got a bit
independent, a hard frost would come
with the fall, and she'd be shed

of the trouble of trimming it back,
she could just plow it under instead.

To Love is to Die
S. K. Epperson

Wickedness is the poison
That invades my soul in moments unsuspecting;
Guaranteed to bring me to my knees
With the pain of guilt and bitter mockery,
That I ever dared believe myself
A being of goodness and worth.

Virtue is the diaphanous cloud
That touches the earth in a virgin's caress,
Ever in sight, yet denying the privilege
Of one lingering embrace,
Leaving me in the shadows,
That I might court and woo,
But remain beneath virtue.

Love is the eternal lesson in humility,
One hand with dagger sharp claws

Shreds the heart, while the other
Soft and smooth, gently strokes,
That I might recognize the beauty of love,
And know the human danger of it.

The Eyes of Love
Sheila O'Shea

These eyes of blue and green, like ice of fire
Strike deep into my soul and make it burn
So caught up in temptation and desire
I do not know which way that I should turn
A face as pale as snow, and eyes as cool
He watches with a wicked, knowing grin
I want to live beneath and break this rule
This torture that consumes me from within
I want what I have never dared to touch
I cannot move, or breathe, or even think
He knows exactly what I want so much
But he will leave me dangling on the brink
And tempt me, taunt me, dragging me through hell
And smiling that cruel smile I love so well

...I shrieked, upstarting —

Deposed, He Remembers Her On the Morning of His Death
Rick Wilber

"Strings, the smallest things," you said,
"how strange they hold such power."
And then your mirrored eyes met mine
as you began that sotto voce hum
and I knew our hour was done.

I recall the tune, a minor thing,
low-keyed and cutely calm
as you sent it past closed painted
lips that had touched my pleasured palm
once tiredly yours.

A small half-heard melodic line
that whispered as you smile —
so like you, love, so virginal a sound
to come as you prepared to strike
at me for ruin and pain.

I know, I know, I realize
our time's gone from us now —
the world has changed and turned
and you have come somehow
to rule us all.

Strings, the smallest things
that move, cause dimensions
to form or die or rise or fall —
modes of vibrations chose red dress
or coal or sun or dust or love
or tepid scorn.

Strings, the smallest things,
define our cosmos by their moves
that choose reality from the nothing
before we all should lose
our agreed little worlds.

You learned how it was done:
a certain drink, a practiced thought,
bought a fulcrum for the task —
to move the smallest things,
these vacuum genesis strings
which form that which probably is.

You and your probable minions
arose from blank nothing to birthe
storms and wrent the earth and conquer
this world's gentle communion.

From strings, the smallest things,
a variant wriggle found force
its outlet to fold gravitic pull
onto our warped fabric
and destroy all that was.

It was ours, no others,
that perfect stringed oscillation
that had formed, so briefly then,
a calm, small place of peace
before chaos, before you
came to lie with me, my love.

Minstrel
Wayne Edwards

pain is strings white strings arctic cold
sharp against the black song of death
the fostered mistress of life
taken because it had no other place
would be meaningless without her

could we live forever cheat
the dawn the one certain dawn
that would otherwise find us
hard and cold as everlasting snow

no
as there is a song of life
its coda must be death
its melody the open eyes of a child
its harmony the somber throaty croon
of the coffin's narrow house

Death Takes a Friend
Virginia Baker

"Cretan," I said, and he laughed,
a song of delight that wavered
black and gold over my fresh grave.

"How would you like it?" he asked,
as though one lump or two would do.
"I came to tea," I said, and he poured me
a wine, thick and red, and smiled,

handed me the cup. "Tragedy is so perverse.
I thought to spare you — what?—
a fire. Drowning, perhaps. A beating
by your friends. Some wild animal

dining on the bones and blood that made you.
You've had no shriek in the night, no tearing
at your throat by knives or vicious teeth.
My last customer saw a werewolf. Once."

My shiver rippled the red in my cup.
"I thought we were —"
"Friends? Of course," he said. "But why
do you worry? Maggots must also eat,

as you have often dined on long-dead flesh,"
and I, I cleared my throat to say, "Your invitation
was macabre — more than I expected on so
bright a day," and he, he only smiled,

held out his hand. I asked his price and did not wince
at the cost of crossing Styx, but asked
what manner my death would be.
He gave no answer, but only turned

in his consummate silence, and tipped
his roiling crown in rakish gesture on his head.
I thought no more to chide him on his manners.

Beaters In The Bush
David Memmott

He is my shadow
he rises to meet me noon and night
I try to hold him at arm's length
but a cold upwelling of animal urge possesses me
drives me from my room out into the street

Hypnotic drumbeat
    quickens the shape
    my dream will take,
        a dream of descending

Jungle fever
driving me before it
    like a killer cat rabid with the odor of man
    seeking sanctum from the flush and cacaphony

    of beaters in the bush

driving me before it
    flotsam in the breaking wave
    driven high on the shore
    discarded armor of the hermit crab
    in a battlefield of small indifferences
    ground to a white powder in the sand

So who will care about another victim,
    another headline in yesterday's news?
I will release them, let them escape
    this oppressive gravity!

David Memmott

I tremble on long, spidery legs
    with anticipation, a razor's edge
        at the throat of night
    feelers twitching in air
    faceted eyes
        magic mirrors without light

driving me before it
driving me down and dirty
    riding the high heels of a woman
    alone on the street
    a woman's worst imagining
    suddenly real.

I watch from my deliberate deadend
    as he rips and tears
        laying her sweet temple to ruin
        freeing her from any dream of descending
        keeping her pure and chaste

Her muffled scream
    along with a thousand others in raw unison
    drummed from this maze of concrete

    rescued from beaters in the bush

    driving us
down the long long alley
before the dawn

...a demon's that is dreaming...

The Old Warlock's Reverie:
a pantoum
Neil Gaiman

Shrieking shapes that stalk the night,
I can hear them scream and moan:
Fox or wolf, they love or fight,
And I wait here on my own.

I can hear them scream and moan:
Clench my nails into my palms —
And I wait here on my own,
Pondering forgotten charms.

Clench my nails into my palms.
— Where's the girdle made of pelt?
Pondering forgotten charms:
— Where's my lycanthropic belt?

Where's the girdle made of pelt?
Did she burn it, steal it, hide it?
Where's my lycanthropic belt?
(Never knock it till you've tried it.)

Did she burn it, steal it, hide it?
— pour myself some wormwood gin —
Never knock it till you've tried it;
Trying too much does you in

Pour myself more wormwood gin,
Blessed drunkenness eludes me.
Trying too much does you in,
True, but just a little soothes me.

Blessed drunkenness eludes me.
Once, beneath the moon, we ran,
True, (but just a little soothes me)
Wolf or fox or cat or man.

Once, beneath the moon, we ran.
That was then. She has not aged.
Wolf or fox or cat or man,
Shapes in which our love we waged...

That was then, she has not aged,
And the pale moon discovers
Shapes in which our love we waged —
Now she shares with other lovers.

And the pale moon discovers
Shrieking shapes that stalk the night.
Now she shares, with other lovers,
Fox or wolf, they love, or fight.

The Kiss: Wounds in the Mouth
Jonathan Vos Post

Wounds in the mouth are hardest to heal, the ice
freezing in narrow gaps is expanding apart
propagating at the speed of breaking glass
rocking the ships of mind in the gated port.

In the cargo's quarters there in the pitching hull
the shadows bulge with the joint-forced carton's squeal
in the corridors of blood & the shapeless hall
with the squall-streaked grime & the promise of lull.

The stays crack like glaciers, the beams give moan
& the bulkheads buckle with a wooden oath
the timbers ache with twisting & they lean
to the spars & deck, bent like ribs to the breath
& the hatches gape at the fury cast in brine
as the storm comes in with its teeth, teeth, teeth.

Awakening
Scott H. Urban

Bringing her in last night, they placed her so
      Her eyes, catching the morning sun,
      Would awaken to the town dressed in dun.
And as the cocks, rustling, began to crow,
She would see, from afar, her home and know
      Within her folk huddled close, as if one,
      Now fearing that their daughter's life was done.
Only then would her tears begin to flow.

For as rough, coarse hands pulled her from the view
      She would see walls and bars, grim and black,
As the screams inside her mounted and grew.
      This, more painful than the screws or the rack:
That last sight of her home — all hope now through —
      And the knowledge she can never go back.

Holocaust In Rosary
Charles A. Gramlich

    Wet eyes in a darkness holy shine
carapace of paint
on apostle faces
    silk wine on scaled dry throats

    comes trailing psalm
      crucifix of cold
      leper-winter

voices in scripture dance grief
fingers crying on ribbed beads
    of ivory

dirge

    church awash in chalice roses
blackened petals
no one kneels
    incubus mouths shriek prophecy

    fingers crawl epistles
      mimes in blood
      scalpel-words

sick in the light the faces melt
grow halos of prismed spikes
    for god

lost

    one mouth with fossil tongue
    speaks of sweet christ dying
    of holocaust in rosary

Pray

Darkness there and nothing more.

Reliquarian Heart
Sandra J. Lindow

So you won't forget
I would imprint my face on your shoulder
Like the Shroud of Turin,
Lines of my features
Glowing faintly like snail trails,
For I cannot forget.
You bloom in my mind like stigmata;
Memories pierce my reliquarian heart
Like splinters of the True Cross,
Impaling me with impossible thoughts,
Hologrammatic angels
Who pause to stare reproachfully
As they tap dance on a neural pinhead.
Loving you was an indulgence I paid and paid,
A Pilgrimage gone astray
On a tollroad far from home.
I would dig the touch of your hands
From beneath my nails
Like dark sand from the Via Dolorosa
And grind it beneath my accelerating heel,
Taking the freeway home from St. Paul.

Judas Nailed His Mouth Open
Charles A. Gramlich

With prayers unanswered and wine grown cold
Judas nailed his mouth open with screams
in a stone petaled darksmare
fed with worms

On a nocturnal crucifix of hate
his limbs crossed and shattered
by the scouring teeth of saints
Judas nailed wide his lips and tongue

While aching flagellant thoughts
danced in currents on his brow
the ankle whips and bone-skin drums
sounded as spikes to tired wounds

The silver was heavy in his mouth
pouring as urine from his tears
swollen like bad meat in his belly
crusts of old scars were weeping

The bats of his sins took flight
foam at their sweetened lips
thorns in their wings to pierce his ears
and dance in a place all rotten with pain

with rope so strong in sick dead light
Judas hung himself with his mouth open
in shrieking red-tipped pain
but did not die

the teeth of him are old that fed the night

The Day of Hitler's Birth
Lisa Lepovetsky

In the synagogue, over the rabbi's head
the eternal flame burns red, cracks its bowl,
and the walls of the ark rattle on hinges
and nails that scream. The warnings of God quake
on parchment hidden behind carved oak doors.
Praying heads bob like buoys before a storm.

Children suck the corners of prayerbooks, ink
and paper disintegrating on their tongues,
and women weep silently, tasting blood in the air.
Something heavy slides across the roof, knocking
slate tiles loose to shatter below like the dreams
of those huddled inside, waiting for the voice of God.

In the Schwarzwald
Lawrence Schimel

They take her brother to break her pride.
She tears splinters from the barracks bed
to still the hunger that gnaws inside.

Through the iron gate, past the words:
Arbeit Macht Frei, she watches guards
throw loaves of bread to the birds.

Not even famine can make barbed wire
seem a candy house she could devour.
The guard tells her: *Child, climb into the fire*.

Gretel tells the guard: *Show me how*.
The open door casts a red shadow
on the trail of ash that leaves Dachau.

The Density of Death
Jonathan Vos Post

Death enters the Physics Laboratory
meanders past the magnets' poles
wires coil on spools and rolls
the slide projector stops its story

Darkness diffracts through sharp-edged prisms
sweeps across oscilloscopes
blackens textbooks' indexed hopes
and silences their catechisms

An airless breeze turns supercool
as volt-ohmmeter's needle dips
the teeth of the alligator clips
are clenched unopening and cruel

Not vacuum tubes that hold their breath
nor manuals for engineers
erase from blackboards of our fears
the chalky fingerprints of Death.

By Nectarine Gate
Steve Sneyd

Shadow slipped past night
guard, cloaked sweetness he sought; mouth
found his full of dust

Satan is a Mathematician
Keith Allen Daniels

for Ambrose Bierce

The tattoo demon laughed.
"I shall inscribe you with *pi* —
a pi whose digits are fractal glyphs
of transcentental agony, whose serifs
are *inflourescent* with infinities.
And I shall render it with all
the panache of a *pointillest*
creating continua from the *discreet*.
But where to begin? The umbilicus
or the anus? The alpha or the omega?"

"Hey, wait a minute!" cried
the mathematician, and the demon
raised an eyebrow. "Pi's an irrational number
with a nonrepeating decimal.
Such a task would take an eternity!"

"Imagine that," said the demon,
and smiling smugly, it poised a talon
tapering to a single atom, plucked lint
from the navel of its flinching victim.

Playing his last card, the mathematician
rose up on his elbow. "Have you really
thought about this? When the flesh
of one man emblazoned subsumes the infinite,
you will have modeled God from numbers
and I will destroy you!"

The other eyebrow twiched. "Well, then,
I shall adorn you with the *closest
rational approximation* of pi."

"Shit!" said the mathematician.

"As you wish," replied the demon,
and began with the anus.

Blood-Crossed Lawyer
Margaret B. Simon

They are becoming soft, their veins
sunken deep in flaccid skin as if
repelling my advances; Camilla lies
upon the coverlet, her ivory arms
embrace the dark Juaquin...

her skin, blue-webbed, transparent —
for a moment, I hesitate, then grant
them one last kiss, for they have
met my stipulations. Tonight, they'll rest,
though my price is always high.

Before the sunrise, I shall bury them
in fine linen, and bind them
tenderly with golden chains;
even now as I prepare, I sense
yet another clandestine affair
in the suite below the window.

Fresh clients! Tomorrow, I'll arrange
a visit and propose my terms for silence.

The Resurrection Man
James S. Dorr

Although "the Anatomy of Man is an ancient and royal subject of study"...it was pursued until quite recently amid surroundings of a most unregal character.
   —James Moores Ball, M.D., **The Body Snatchers**
   (Dover Books, 1989)

Beware the Resurrection Man
If ye'd be buried in yer grave
Tae rest in peaceful-like repose,
'Cause Edinburgh be filled wi' men
Like Burke an' Hare an' a' their kin
Tae dig ye up soon's ye be laid
An' scarcely stiff wi' in yer box
Where ye micht *think* ye sleeps in God.
But others knows there's silver made
Upon yer corse — aye, silver earned
An' also gold upon men's bones
Delivered fresh tae Surgeons an'
Their unco' ilk wha' asks nae askin's,
Pays instead wha' ere's tae gi'
Tae cut an' slice an' tak' yer guts
Tae tie in clumps. An' wha's tae save
Ye once ye're planted 'neath the ground? —
Nae patent coffin, lined in iron,
Nor steel-barred *Morte-safe*
Dulls the tools *these* butchers wield
Upon yer worn flesh as ye lie
Entabled, stretched upon yer back,
While they above, they tweaks yer eyes,
They twists yer nose an' they pickles yer brains
These Resurrectionists' customers do —

Sae *beware, beware,* as best ye can,
An' wha'e're in life ye else micht gain,
An' wha'e're prayers ye may pray still be sure
Tae beware the Resurrection Man!

The Monster's Mother
Mary A. Turzillo

It shouldn't surprise you
how, born out of her mother Mary's death,
growing up in that household with Doctor Polidori,
running away with her silly genius Shelley,
(for which his wife drowned herself in the Serpentine),
she would have written the tortured romance
about a mishapen thing born from a man,
all those murdered children,
the anguish of a monster without a mate,
because, after all, maybe she could see
down the aisle of years
to the babies that died in her arms
while she tried to nurse life back into them,
her husband killed by cold water,
and little Percy, the baby that lived,
so hard for her to keep
when his wicked grandparents
tried to rip him out of her life.
It shouldn't surprise us at all
given the scars on her heart
that in her teenage thriller,
the one she pittied the most
was the monster.

The Dead Who Do Not Sleep Under Green Street
Steve Rasnic Tem

The dead, too tired to rest, too sad to pray,
do not sleep in town, do not sleep under green.
The life they have in dreams must stay.

They have no skill at counting, no word for the day,
cannot leave this street, cannot keep it clean:
the dead, too tired to rest, too sad to pray.

The gray smoke gathers: dead children at play.
The missing hear their mothers but are not seen.
The life that have in dreams must stay.

In Green Street nights the houses sway.
Near dark corners, under dim lights lean
the dead, too tired to rest, too sad to pray.

The husband weeps where the dead wife lay,
in his bed 'til morning she whispers unseen.
The life she has in dreams must stay.

The dead who do not sleep have much to say,
of loves unanswered, of lives between.
The dead, too tired to rest, too sad to pray:
the life they have in dreams must stay.

The Ghost of Anchises: a Poem
Based on an Old Story English Teachers Know about an Ancient Roman Who Tried Three Times to Hug his Dead Father

Donald M. Hassler

We struggled at the undertaker's when
Those golden playing fields where all our dads
Had played out their youth in olden days
Had to be recalled in detail. Memory,
In fact, became Vergil's hell for us
And three of us three times tried to hug the ghost
Of actual dates and actual wins. Earlier
I had watched my brother in the middle
Of the night bend quietly beside the body
And kiss our father, the father of our wives.
Many fathers and many sons were embodied
In that near embrace. The women, stronger perhaps,
Had gone huddling off to collect themselves.
So we were left with barren memory,
And Bobby's simple bending focused
Then for me those shadowy embraces from Anchises
Through the other fathers we have lost
To the continual embrace of fading memories
And lost traditions. Since we shall never hold
Our athletic dads again, we clutch their gold
And read these poems that seem so strange and old.

Captain Royate Montgomery Writes Home
Thomas E. Fuller

My Darling Wife
I take pen in hand once again to write and hope that this missive finds you well.

> *I do not know this place. There are no undulating plains in Virginia, no fortification riddled mountains in Georgia.*

The weather here continued to be fine.

> *The fogs come early and stay late. The clouds never leave. The moon is an empty blind eye, the sun a memory.*

The men are in good spirits in spite of the short supplies we must endure.

> *We are ghosts haunting an empty land, hurling across the grasslands on steeds that never tire.*

We have no seen any Yankees in several days although we have had indications of their presence.

> *Other armies are glimpsed at a distance, marching battalions of shifting smoke. I do not know their standards. Do they know ours?*

Our days are spent foraging and preparing for the next battle. We are constantly vigilant.

> *We followed the shadow of a hulking land ironclad yesterday. There was a faded red star on its upper works and it stank of hot oil and spent gunpowder.*

Mail is very irregular. I live for your letters and treasure them all.

The faded paper comes apart at the folds and the treasured words scurry around like ink spiders.

I love you with all my heart and soul.

I ravage my memories but I can no longer remember your face only images of onyx and ivory and lace.

Your loving husband, Royate

The fog has broken and the bugles scream. I look at my hand and it is the same color as my uniform.

Down and Away (My Queen)
G. Warlock Vance

Down down to
Murky depths I
Go submerged
In cold cold
Kissing me frost
And icicle bright
Felicity felia
Regina don't run
Don't go leave me
Dark and tear-stained
Face when night's
Descent has bent
My head bright
Icicles hang in
Tear-ducts mine
And swoon oh
Kiss me my
Black plague and
Fear away away
And on anon —

Night Call
John B. Rosenman

The phone rang
and I answered.
My father's death
sang to me through the wires.

From California to Virginia
circuits thrummed.
My father died
somewhere over New Mexico

telling me not to give up
on that third strike
but swing
be a man,
hold the BB gun steady —
died
and left me my mother's voice
crackling like static
3,000 miles away,
telling me what I already knew:

a coronary
stab of pain
one last disappointed thought
of me

then nothing.

When It All Began
Robert Frazier

...is what you'll want to know, I mean
like who was the first victim and how did it start

are the questions you'll ask me one day
under maximum security, when it goes down,

when the trail of clues leads you inexorably
to some fly-specked, peeling, nicotine yellow dive

where I'm eating cold oatmeal or catching reruns
of *The Fugitive* and *Invasion of the Body Snatchers*

just trying to distract myself, desperate by-holy-mother-of-god
to distract myself from this run-on psychobabble

that funnels through my head, and then you'll hammer down
the door, snap my arms behind me, stamp my face

into the grain of the floor and treat me like I couldn't possibly
understand the true gravity of what I have done,

but I know, oh, don't kid yourself, I've lived more than you can
imagine, seen more real estate burn in the flickering depths

of all those eyes up close before they turned dull,
and that's what you'll be afraid of and fascinated with

when you get the tape recorders rolling, buttons clicking,
heads crackling, magnetic ribbons gathering miles of my voice,

and you'll begin to pick at my brain for the details,
and I'll start somewhere near the beginnning for you,

oh, not all the way back to how Dad used to cold cock me
when he'd drained his fifth or two of JD,

or how I'd get locked in the shed out in the back field
with leaky cans of thinner that made my head swim

with muddy scenarios for revenge, unrequited revenge,
and no, definitely not about how the Stranger found me,

that bloody monster found me unconscious by the thinner,
how he melded minds with me before he died,

how he hoped the communion would cleanse us both,
instead of driving me pure bug-ugly B-A-D,

and certainly not a bit about the subsequent pleasure
I took in living these opposites, in between some

screwed-up metaphorical punishment for man's sins,
or at least the sins of dumb shit alcoholic Swede truckers

and that sweetness I find in the no-holds-barred mind rage
that engulfs me, whether you call it that or a different word,

christ, I'll jump past all this because I can't chance
that some wuss of a social worker might get his lather up

about my mistreatment being a Cause, about Downtrodden Men
that can't be held Responsible, because I won't tell you

that I don't deserve what I deserve, I do, so I'll give the world
exactly what they expect, the whole opening hook

about how my name is Jesse Nordquist, Scandinavian blond-boy
born in Iowa, in the heartland of the American reich,

how I feel no remorse nor can I hardly remember anything
but those details, those sweet and fascinating moments

from the scrapbooks of Hell;
you see, the first time, well, it was an accident,

sort of, since I'd only meant to peep on this chick
that worked at the sandwich shop in downtown Des Moines,

Robert Frazier

just followed her to her back street third floor apartment,
hiding on the fire escape in a light rain while she stripped

from her work uniform, stripped slow for the mirror,
running her hands down that Italian silk slip of hers,

like mother used to when she tried Dad with a pleading look,
I mean who'd have thought this chick would then

slip out onto the landing to light a cigarette, just catch me
in the brickwork shadows, and say the wrong thing,

recognizing me out loud as the kid who hung around eating subs,
and if she hadn't pressed my hand to the pure heat of her breast,

oh the musk of this girl mingled with rain water and the cloying exhaust
of the city, if she hadn't then pushed me away laughing,

laughing until I had to choke it off, had to end that mocking sound
like the sound Dad had made when he volleyballed my head,

me crying and unable to stand the laugh echoing inside me, then who
knows, who knows for sure, I mean *whoa*, you better believe

you'll have enough to analyze with that one alone, though, afterwards,
all the unclosed books and down-and-dirty investigative spooks

in the country will want the absolute and unexpurgated nine yards,
simply said, the way it turned into something huge and malevolent

and unearthly in my brain, tumorous, a drug jolt
run-on full metal tilt scream of power I couldn't turn off,

and the way I covered my tracks with waitresses in Iowa City and
Council Bluffs and Dubuque, innocents named Maria or Claudia,

thus establishing the supposed seriality of my nature,
so I could then bail out, never eat a pizza again out of fear,

of a sense of reformation, yet suddenly to find I had become
what I pretended—that I enjoyed it, the taking,

with a penchant, actually, for boys, though not with
any deviant motivations, more in a have-mercy-on-them

run-on mind set, you know, don't let them suffer,
put the little buggers out of their misery, its best

to just find them and ease their pain, like that Protestant kid
I did in where was it, Anacortez, Washington,

whose parents raised him in the basement, like a mushroom,
he'd never seen the light until I carried him out on the lawn at noon

and let him blind himself with the sun before I liberated him,
not that I was some sort of saint for this act,

I knew mercy but also there were kids I just snuffed on first sight,
assuming their lives to be miserable as must every child's be

by their mere fate of being born, and I did all this because...
because nobody eased mine, my pain, damn it, nobody ever cared

about mine, nobody, get my drift, well as a result,
I became the kind of nameless drifter you can't follow

with a road map, you'd shred the thing with push pins or mark it
silly with red trails and blue trails and green dotted lines, but,

but if you could trace murder that well, like I said, it would finally
lead to a cockroach motel in, say, Nadatenango, the mythic town

where all jaded travelers seem to end their journeys,
and no road begins to further lands,

or perhaps back in Iowa, hey, by some great twist of fate
it might be in that very Italian girl's apartment,

employing the clever sort of twist I sometimes devise
to keep myself from going stir-#!*?ing crazy, yes,

but no matter I'd be had, so then we'd get down to the details folks,
wouldn't we, transferred to a room with no windows,

maximum detainment, those soul-sucking recorders humming,
the details like my name being Jesse Nordquist, yeah,

born the son of a truck driver in Mount Vernon, Iowa,
all of it because that's all you really want, you, you could care less

about justice, capital J justice, really, you just want to stand there
like a fire watcher, you know, that breed of passerby

that stops for auto accidents, riveted by all that's bloody and
energized with the moment and filled with the great passions of life,

of love, with the ringing gong of death, just standing there
like it was four-color video entertainment,

Just The Sweet Details, Sir; and finally my telling you
there's only one way to turn it off, man,

ending this blurred-together dynamo of fury
contained in my skull this Parasite this living *presence*

just one and final solution when
you've at last had your fill of fascination

my name is Jesse just no hesitation
no small hypocritical prayer for my lost soul

just put that hand on the power switch please
please one way out for us all us all us all us all

just pull it please PLEASE my name is jesse
we'll all find out exactly when

it ends if it can ever ever ever end...

Jeffrey Dahmer
S. P. Somtow

Death is a little pinprick. Just a jab.
Nothing to fear. No suffering. No pain
Compared to the stern, stupefying stab
Of loneliness. Some acid to the brain
Will melt away that lingering abhorrence;
Then, all at once, by fiat from above,
Transcendence; for we'll taste tempestuous torrents
Of desire. For you, eternal love;
For me, mere transience; for I consume
And what was beautiful becomes old bones
And flesh, and rots in a suburban room,
While your response to my perfervid moans
Is not to speak at all. Oh stay, oh stay —
Not like to rest — True love does not decay!

Falling
Lee Ballentine

The sky glows—fine gold is falling on the town
whose people stand—watch—listen to the sound.

Their children run barefooted in the lane
and are not frightened so they feel no pain.

Run till they tire and their feet become
too heavy for a child to lift
and then they stop and watch the stuff to see it drift.

Bells to the ear go silent the seconds creep
for these ones who are sliding into sleep
and then their gazing up—the dusting down
of careless powder will preserve each frown...

Cover the outstretched arm and gild the thigh
palm of the hand and surface of the upturned eye.

My Body Goes on Forever
G. Warlock Vance

My body will burn
Bright scintillation
Lances through the
Night falls cold
And darkness tries
To wrap me up in-
To an ebon womb
Consumed by flame
The black shell shall
Remain until the
Carbon break-down dis-
Illusion some con-
Fusion where we go
But neat to know
Our light bright
Bodies burning goes
Out but on forever.

The Suicide
S. K. Epperson

The snow doesn't touch her;
Death's embrace is her shield,
Her shelter.
She sleeps unaware.
It is I who shiver,
My skin that feels the bite
Of cold. And knowing.
I fear for her,
She who sleeps,
And doesn't feel the snow.

In The Blindness of the Hour
Mark Rich

In the blindness of the hour when the blind worm sings
and the crow's wing crawls quiet across the coiling sky,
when I wait for you amid the sleeping midnight blooms
in this deeply shadowed land well known to you and me;

when the blind worm sings of what the greyed grave-walker brings
to slumberers fast asleep where none living will lie,
in the cold and echoing fastness of worm-worn tombs
well-worn and known, where I wait for you, and you for me;

when in the blindness of blindest hour the worm sings
and night's quiet falls over every unquiet mind
and souls invisibly flit on weightless, sightless wings:
then, *then*, the late-night wanderers will stumble and find

the somber land rising from grave-damp soil, which will be
ours, well-worn and well-known, where I find you, and you, me.

The Dreams Within His Dream
Michael N. Langford

for Victoria

Discovered deep within near-comatose delirium,
poor Edgar Poe's slight forty-year-old frame,
clothed in dark mantle quintessential,
with his back against the seeming Final Door,
in that Baltimore doorway in 1849,
came to taste the cool, earthy night of premature
burial on the churchyard's back pew
for but a few years.

And though the interred might have much better used
the honorarium much prior to the interment,
a curious classroom fund — collected from
many and many a child caught loving that corpse —
found loving with a love that was more than love —
finally financed the revisionist excavation
for the more prominent relocation of his renewed reputation.

Yet how conquered was the Conqueror Worm's
presumptuous imposition of that ultimate decomposition
during the composer's temporary subterranean disposition!

The corpse in question, on the contrary, exhibited
such a striking reliquification

of its formerly placid putrification —
such a surprising suppleness
of its earlier crumbling decadence —
that the student assemblage began
shaking the remains and calling its name,
much as a crowd of cherubim might have
aided the angel Israfel in summoning Lazarus,
by gently slapping the face of Death
and announcing some ancient breakfast is served
on the Dead Sea's own Plutonian Shore.

Lashes colored midnight quivered
as ebon eyes opened to new light.
Yet not a minute stopped or stayed he,
but, with mien of lord in quest of lady,
strode off into the night forevermore.

Because she could not stop for Death,
Poe kindly stopped for Emily.
The carriage carried just those two
into the alabaster citadel of Solitude,
the hideous habit of the veil.

On a rainy street in Prague, Edgar munched his lunch and
leaned upon the bars of Kafka's cage.
Admiring the hunger-artist's proud devotion to his art,
Poe thrust the crust of the staff of Death-in-Life
into a bevy of black birds nearby.

John Allan's stepchild waited hours in the Martian midday
with unflagging, ticket-clenching anticipation,
for the splendid cyber-rejuvenation
of Roderick Usher's horrific habitation.
Tour courtesy of Ray's trolley-driving imagination.

Michael N. Langford

Then voyaging, ever voyaging across the ages,
finally abandoning the prodigal Life,
finally defying his tormentor Loss,
finally forsaking his damned bitch-mistress Decay,
the Philosopher of Composition enters within himself —
within his own dearest realm —
and finds landfall upon a planet populated with Poes.

A visionary palace haunted by children cloned
with seed distilled from locks of his hair
presented to girls in his youth.
And — Ah, Psyche! — conjured from Virginia's own dust!
A multitude of offspring cavorting in the farthest flung
kingdom by the Sea of Night,
well away from all covetous denizens
writhing in narrow celestial bitterness.
Every maid an Annabel and every boy an Eddie,
where thirteen moons beam, bringing lifetime's of dreams,
and a billion stars shine in a million dark eyes.

Though all are but the dreams within his Dream,
Poe lastly comes to know himself as but
the Poe within his progeny.

Eagerly I wished the morrow...

The White Worm
On the Death of Virginia Poe, by Consumption
James S. Dorr

Poor Eddie! Flecks once more have stained the pillow
where I lay my head, pretending sleep. The sheets
so white are marked with red. I think, I dream
as Eddie might of that within — the Killer Worm! —
that ravishes so white, so heartless, my poor heart,
that bores its way through lung and flesh, and thus
consuming all! My breath! My life — my breath.
I fight to gain just one more draught of air,
to have my chest expand once more with boiling,
dragging breath that bubbles as through fire —
a rasp! a groan! — as I seek one more day
to hold his hand in mine. He sits at my
bedside while in me, yes, I see the Worm
Triumphant, boring still its way — my weight
is down. In childhood, once, I was robust
though never large. I was a healthy girl,
but now my Eddie lifts me for my needs
as if a feather lay between these pale,
streaked sheets. I feel the chill again as cold
fights fever, as I glow, once searing flame,
then ice. I see the mirror, how my cheeks
are flushed, my forehead pallid, as I sip
the water Eddie brings to cool my throat.
And in myself I see a tomb of ghouls
lie dormant, waking to the White Worm's call,
to eat, to chew both flesh and soul. And lung —
I drown in my own blood! — and always, always,
one breath more I struggle to receive,
one memory more. I was, and am, a child
as well as wife. I married young to Eddie

as I die now, young as well, though I recall
the love we had — my poet Poe and I —
and think of worms, yes, horrors that *he* face
with me beside him, poverty and worse,
but still —
       I cough again. *What will my Eddie do
when I am gone?* But still I think of summers
past, of *garden* worms, of Eddie's cat,
of grass and flowers and us amid them. Eddie's
working late at night, so quiet not
to stir my rest. The poems he wrote, the tales
as well of doomed, lost loves, and yet I think —
another breath, another half-lung's fill
of air! — the Worm grows stronger in my heart
and yet, as I sink back, exhausted, still
I know *our* love endured — and will! I know.
I dream. I think. I squeeze his hand as he
knows too that Death, the Master Worm, is here
within this room, this 'poverished shack, and yet
I think of life, of joy. For all we were
not rich — poor Eddie struggled always for
our sustenance, our clothes, our very food —
but, ah! the years we had, though short, were good.

And my soul from out that shadow...

One Crow, Many Graves
Dwight E. Humphries

Just inside the city graveyard,
A crow sounds a corvine sermon
To the motionless dead; perched
In a leaf-shorn oak, he creates
His song, his croak to fleshless
Skeletons whose names are not
Important in the long scheme
Of things. In this mid-winter,
I doubt the once cherished bones
Will quicken and warm, beyond
Reach of all life but where
All life shall come, and the
Messenger of Odin makes his moan
Across a vale and small hills
Which are a final home.

Eventually, the swart bird will too
Join those he exhorts, for every
Existence is doomed to cease, the
Quick hasten through the months
And years to finally lie still,
Where they fell or else gathered,
And cherished for memory's brief
Span — in time one becomes the
Anonymous dead despite what tomb
We inhabit; the graved stones
Which mark mortal shipwreck are
Erased by rain and the acid
Gnawing of temporality, time
Which flow on, yet life continues
And more fall with each passing

Year. At some point, flesh decays,
Bereft the cunning spark which is
Life, animating what in the end
Is a loathsome corpse.

It almost seems the black bird
Mocks, but such is not so, for it
Too shall be brought low; all
Life dances, twitches to an
Appointed end, making way for
The wheel to turn and begin
Again. Still, the harsh song
Has a desolate note, the obsidian
Feathered thing shall grate the
Very air; but none in those solemn,
Private places hear, brains
Which could be swayed are gone,
And the dry reefs which are
Skeletons are attuned for a
Far, far different song.

"Nevermore."

Once upon a Midnight... has been printed in a limited edition of 950 copies, of which 750 have been bound in softcover. 200 sets of unbound sheets are to be held in reserve to be bound in a hardcover omnibus edition of The Unnameable Poetry Works. This book has been printed on 65# booktext natural which is acid-free for longevity. The type has been set in Times New Roman. The "Raven" quotations are in Monotype Corsiva. Midnight... was printed and bound in Virginia.